spot

CREEPY CRAWLIES

WASPS

by Nessa Black

AMICUS | AMICUS INK

stinger

wings

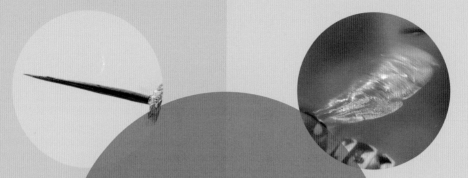

Look for these
words and pictures
as you read.

nest

queen

Buzz! Buzz!
There is a wasp.

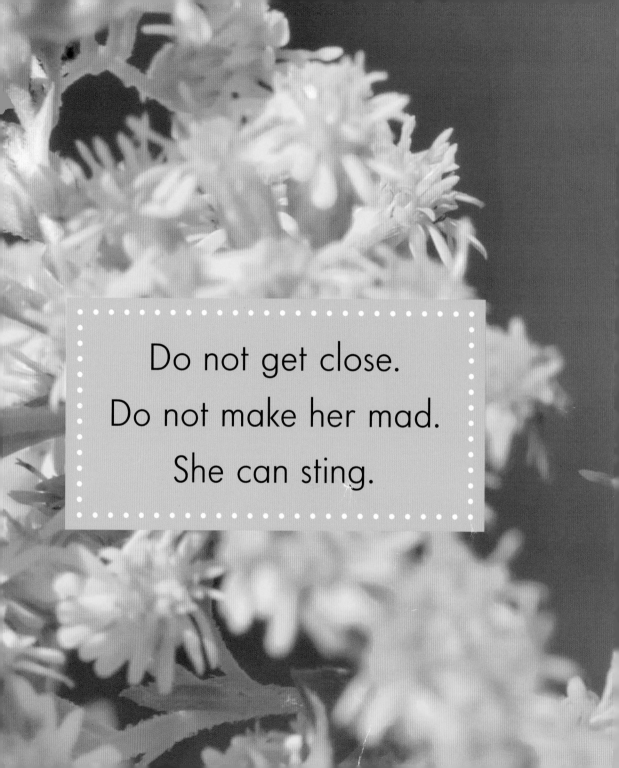

Do not get close.
Do not make her mad.
She can sting.

stinger

Look at her stinger.

It is sharp.

Only a female can sting.

wings

Look at their wings.
They beat fast.
They make a buzzing sound.

nest

Look at the nest.
Wasps build it themselves.
It is a home for the colony.

queen

Look at the queen.
She is bigger than the others.
She lays the eggs.

A wasp is helpful.
It eats bugs
that eat plants.

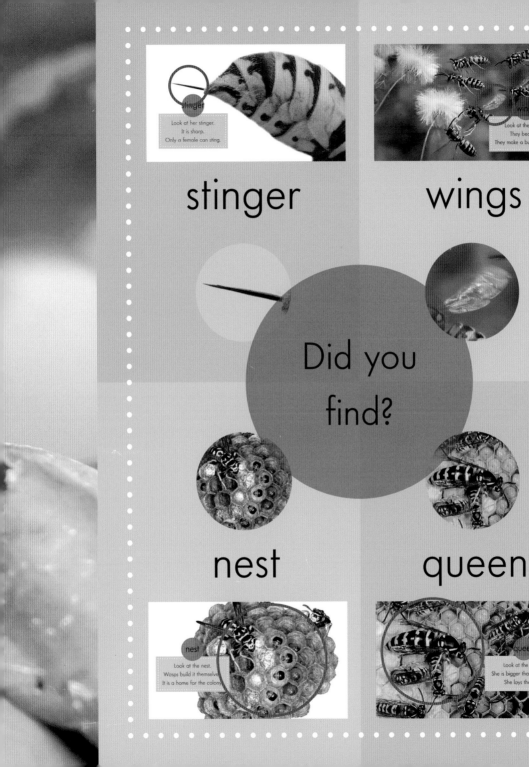

stinger

Look at her stinger.
It is sharp.
Only a female can sting.

wings

Look at their wings.
They beat fast.
They make a buzzing sound.

Did you find?

nest

Look at the nest.
Wasps build it themselves.
It is a home for the colony.

queen

Look at the queen.
She is bigger than the others.
She lays the eggs.

Spot is published by Amicus and Amicus Ink
P.O. Box 1329, Mankato, MN 56002
www.amicuspublishing.us

Library of Congress Cataloging-in-Publication Data
Names: Black, Nessa, author.
Title: Wasps / by Nessa Black.
Description: Mankato, MN : Amicus/Amicus Ink, [2019] |
  Series: Spot. Creepy crawlies | Audience: K to grade 3.
Identifiers: LCCN 2017049951 (print) | LCCN 2017052843
  (ebook) | ISBN 9781681515793 (pdf) | ISBN
  9781681515410 (library binding) | ISBN 9781681523798
  (pbk.)
Subjects: LCSH: Wasps–Juvenile literature.
Classification: LCC SB945.W3 (ebook) | LCC SB945.W3
  B53 2019 (print) | DDC 595.79–dc23
LC record available at https://lccn.loc.gov/2017049951

Printed in China

HC 10 9 8 7 6 5 4 3 2 1
PB 10 9 8 7 6 5 4 3 2 1

Wendy Dieker and Alissa Thielges,
  editors
Deb Miner, series designer
Kazuko Collins, book designer
Holly Young, photo researcher

Photos by iStock/2manydogs cover;
Age Fotostock/H. Bellmann/F. Hecker
12–13; iStock/ConstantinCornel 6–7;
Shutterstock/irin-k 1, Lee Hua Ming
3, Paul Reeves Photography 4-5, Irina
Kozorog 8-9, Shishka4 10–11, Dhawan
Dirksen 14

WASPS